So You Want to Be
A Gourmet

So You Want to Be A Gourmet

Floyd J. Hall

Copyright © 2009 by Floyd J. Hall.

ISBN: Hardcover   978-1-4363-7347-0
                 Softcover   978-1-4363-7346-3

All rights reserved. No part of this book may be reproduced or transmitted in any form or by any means, electronic or mechanical, including photocopying, recording, or by any information storage and retrieval system, without permission in writing from the copyright owner.

This book was printed in the United States of America.

To order additional copies of this book, contact:
Xlibris Corporation
1-888-795-4274
www.Xlibris.com
Orders@Xlibris.com

43171

CONTENTS

Acknowledgments 9
Beef Cheese Quiche 11
Beef Log 12
Beef Log Stuffing 12
Beef Stew 13
Bow Tie Pasta, Peppers and Meatballs 14
Breakfast Quesadilla 15
Chicken Pot Pie 16
Cornbread Batter 17
Clam Chowder 18
Coby Cheese & Italian Sausage Stuffed Breast 19
Cuban Beef Kabob 20
Curry Beef & Wild Rice with Mushrooms 21
French Toast 22
Grill Chicken and Oyster Dressing 23
Grilled Salmon with steamed Asparagus Pears and Raspberry Sauce 24
Italian Sausage Calzones 25
Lasagna 26
Momma's Gumbo 27
Rice 28
Moo Goo Gai Pan 28
Pan Grilled Grouper with Avocado Salsa 29
Pizza 30
Portobello Pinwheel 31
Rainbow Trout Stuffed with Oyster Dressing 32
Risotto 33
Scallops & Steamed Bok Choy with Mango Salsa 34
Shepherd's Pie 35
Shrimp Fettuccine Alfredo 36
Shrimp Scampi 37
Spaghetti 38
Stir Fried Beef 39
Stuffed Bell Peppers 40

APPETIZERS

Asian Chicken Fingers 42
Broccoli 43
Daddy's Cheese Ball 43
Egg Rolls 44
Honey Mustard Wings 45
Honey Mustard Wraps 46
Melanie's Coconut Shrimp 47
Onion Rings 48
Sweet Potatoes Fries 49
Stuffed Mushrooms 49
Wontons 50

DESSERT

Apple Pie 52
Green Tomato Pie 53
Jack Daniel's Sweet Potato Pie 54
Mandarin Orange Sorbet 55
Mango Cheesecake 55
Mango Frozen Yogurt 56
Peach Cobbler 56
Peach Pie 57
Pecan Pie 58
Raspberry Cheesecake 59

MARINADES, SAUCES, SALAD DRESSING, ETC ....

Asian Marinade 61
Asian Sauce 61
Asian Wing Sauce 62
Basil Herb Cream Cheese 62
Béchamel Sauce 63
Beef Log Stuffing 63
Beef Marinade 64
Blue Cheese Vinaigrette 64
Blueberry Syrup 65
Blackberry Syrup 65
Chili Oil 66

Creamy Dressing	66
Cuban Garlic Marinade	67
Egg Roll Stuffing	68
Feta Cheese Vinaigrette	69
Garlic Mashed Potato	69
Gravy	70
Honey Mustard Sauce	70
Hot Wing Sauce	71
Italian Sausage Stuffing	71
Italian Sausage, Wild Rice and Garlic Bok Choy Stuffing	72
Lasagna Sauce	73
Mesquite Smoked Salmon Stuffing	74
Mushroom Sauce	74
Oyster Dressing	75
Pesto	76
Pineapple Dipping Sauce	76
Pizza Sauce	77
Pizza Sauce (for calzones only)	78
Raspberry Sauce	79
Seafood and Beef Stuffing	79
Spice Tomatoes	80
Tomato Stuffing	80
Wild Rice & Mushrooms	81
Wing Sauce	81

PIE CRUST, PIZZA DOUGH, ETC . . .

Garlic Rolls	83
Garlic Butter	83
Graham Cracker Crust	84
Pasta Dough	84
Pie Crust, (1 pie crust)	85
Pie Crust, (2 pie crust)	86
Pizza Dough	87

STOCKS

Beef Stock	89
Chicken Stock	89
Shrimp Stock	90

SALSA, DIPS, ETC...

Avocado Salsa	92
Fruit Salsa	92
Mango Salsa	93
Tomato Salsa	93
Seafood Dip	94
Onion Dip	95
Spinach Dip	95

SOUP, SALADS, ETC...

Cheddar Cheese Soup	97
Egg Drop Soup	98
Three Bean Soup	99
Broccoli, Apricot, Almond Salad	100
Fruit Salad	100
Spinach Salad with Feta Cheese Vinaigrette	101
Spinach Salad with Grilled Halibut and Blue Cheese Vinaigrette	102

TOPPINGS

Apple Topping	104
Raspberry Cheesecake Topping	104
Index	105

ACKNOWLEDGMENTS

To My God who made it all possible.

To My Family who allowed me to test many recipes on them.

To Louise Jacobson who worked diligently with me throughout this publication.

To Melissa Hall who once stopped eating to say, "Daddy, this is good."

To Ronald Kyle Cole who stated, "This food is delicious."

To Helen Caldwell, (Moo Goo), for her continuous words of encouragement and her quest for "The Recipe".

To Terri L. Hyatt, MD for her continuous words of encouragement and honest support.

To Dorothy Johnson who once said, "Floyd, I don't like deer but Bambi taste good."

To Nida Williams for her steadfast support and patience.

To Nathan Jones and all of the staff at the Saddle Creek Apple Store for their technical support.

To Lynn Moore and all of the staff at Xlibris Corporation.

To everyone who provided any assistance which expedited this publication into a reality.

BEEF CHEESE QUICHE

6 slices of beef bacon, (cut into 1 inch slices)
¼ cup of onion, diced
¼ cup of bell peppers, diced
¼ cup of mushrooms, sliced
3 garlic cloves, minced
½ cup of ground beef
3 eggs, beaten
½ cup of milk
½ cup of cheddar cheese, shredded
½ cup of mozzarella cheese, shredded
1 teaspoon of sea salt
½ teaspoon of ground black pepper
piecrust, (see index)

Preheat the oven to 350 degrees. (Meanwhile line the pie crust with foil and bake for 10 minutes. Remove the crust from the oven and set aside.)

Place the bacon in a skillet over medium high heat and cook until brown. Remove and set aside. Add onion and sauté for 2 minutes. Add the bell peppers, mushrooms, garlic and sauté 2 additional minutes. Remove the mixture and set aside.

Cook the beef until brown. Drain beef and add to the vegetable mixture. Add bacon and mix well.

In a bowl add eggs, milk, cheese, salt, black pepper and blend well. Add the beef mixture and mix well. Remove foil and pour the mixture into pie crust. Bake for 45 to 50 minutes.

Variations 1) Omit bacon, bell peppers, mushrooms, ground beef, mozzarella cheese and substitute 1 cup of chopped broccoli, use 1 cup of cheddar cheese total. (Sauté the broccoli with the onion for 4 minutes.)

BEEF LOG

1 flank steak, (2 lbs)
2 sheets of plastic wrap
¼ teaspoon of sea salt
¼ teaspoon of ground black pepper
kitchen cord

BEEF LOG STUFFING

Pesto, (see index)
½ cup of pepper jack cheese, shredded
1 small bag of spinach
½ cup of provolone cheese, shredded
2 tablespoons of canola oil

Flatten the flank steak between two sheets of plastic wrap and pound with a meat mallet until about ¼ inch thick. Cut the ends to square the meat. Season both sides of the meat with salt and pepper. Spread a layer of pesto on meat leaving ½ inch borders. Sprinkle with pepper jack cheese, then spinach leaves and top with provolone cheese. Roll the steak into a log. Tie the steak with kitchen cord. (Preheat the oven to 350 degrees.) Place oil in a cast iron skillet over medium high heat. Sear the steak on all sides. Remove and place in the oven. Roast the steak for 20 minutes. Remove and cool for 10 minutes. Cut into ½ inch slices. Garnish each slice with ½ teaspoon of pesto.

BEEF STEW

2 tablespoons of olive oil
1 ½ lbs of round steak, (cut into ½ inch cubes)
2 cups of carrots, diced
3 stalks of celery, diced
1 large onion, diced
6 garlic cloves, minced
1 teaspoon of basil, chopped
1 ½ teaspoon of sea salt
3 large tomatoes, peeled, seeded and diced
4 cups of potatoes, peeled and diced
1 cup of red wine
6 cups of beef stock, (see index)
½ teaspoon of ground black pepper

In a large deep saucepan heat oil and beef cubes together over medium high heat. Sauté for 6 minutes, (or until brown). Remove beef and set aside. Add carrots, celery, onion, garlic and sauté for 5 minutes. Return the beef and cook 1 additional minute. Add basil, 1 teaspoon of salt, tomatoes, potatoes, wine, stock and bring to a boil. Reduce the heat to low and simmer for 90 minutes. Stirring occasionally. Season with ½ teaspoon of salt, and pepper just before serving.

BOW TIE PASTA, PEPPERS AND MEATBALLS

½ small onion, (chopped)
3 garlic cloves, (minced)
3 tablespoons of olive oil
½ lb of ground chuck or sirloin
½ lb of ground pork
1 cup of breadcrumbs
1 cup of chicken stock, (see index)
1 egg
½ teaspoon of sea salt
½ teaspoon of black pepper
¼ teaspoon of cayenne pepper
1 tablespoon of oregano
2 cups of bow tie pasta
1 small red bell pepper, (julienned)
1 small yellow bell pepper, (julienned)
1 cup of button mushrooms, (sliced)
½ cup of white wine, (Zolo Chardonnay)
½ cup of Parmigiano-Reggiano, (grated)

Preheat oven to 350 degrees.

Sauté ½ onion, and garlic together in 1 tablespoon oil over medium high heat until onion is translucent. Remove from heat and set aside.

Mix beef and pork together in a medium size bowl. Add the onion and garlic mixture. Combine breadcrumbs with ½ cup of hot chicken stock. Add soaked crumbs and egg to the beef and pork mixture. Season with salt, black and cayenne pepper. Add oregano. Use a tablespoon and scoop small portions. Roll into small balls. Pan-fry balls until brown in a cast iron skillet. Remove, drain, and place meatballs into the oven. Bake for 10 minutes and remove.

Cook pasta according to the directions, strain, remove and set aside.

In a large saucepan add 2 tablespoons of oil and bell peppers. Sauté for 3 minutes over medium high heat. Add mushrooms and cook for 4 minutes. Add ½ cup of chicken stock, and white wine. Bring to a boil. Reduce the heat to low. Add meatballs, pasta and simmer for 10 minutes. Remove from heat, sprinkle with cheese and serve immediately.

BREAKFAST QUESADILLA

4 eggs
2 tablespoons of milk
2 tablespoons of olive oil
1 tablespoon of butter
¼ cup of red bell peppers, (diced)
¼ cup of scallions, (diced)
8 flour tortillas (6 inches)
8 slices of cheddar cheese
¼ teaspoon of sea salt
¼ teaspoon of ground black pepper
tomato salsa, see index

Beat eggs and milk together and set aside. Heat the oil and butter together in a saucepan over medium high heat until melted. Add bell peppers and sauté for 2 minutes. Add scallions and sauté for 2 additional minutes. Pour the egg mixture into saucepan and scramble lightly. Season with salt and pepper. Remove from the heat and set aside.

Place a tortilla in a clean saucepan over medium heat. Put 1 slice of cheese on the tortilla. Pour 1/4 of the egg mixture over the cheese. Top with 1 slice of cheese and a second tortilla. Cook for 2 minutes, press lightly and turn over. Cook for 3 minutes and remove. Cut into 8 sections. Prepare additional quesadillas. Serve immediately with tomato salsa.

CHICKEN POT PIE

1 tablespoons of cornstarch
1 cup of chicken broth, (see index)
2 cups of baked chicken, diced
1 can of diced carrots, (14-16 oz) drained
1 can of butter beans, (14-16 oz) drained
1 can of whole kernel corn, (14-16 oz) drained
1 can of sweet peas, (14-16 oz) drained
cornbread batter, (see index)

Preheat the oven to 400 degrees.

In a medium size bowl combine the first two ingredients and set aside. Place chicken in the bottom of a large deep baking dish. Add a layer of carrots, beans, corn and peas. Pour on the broth mixture. Top with cornbread batter. Bake for 20 minutes or until bread is golden brown.

Variations 1) Substitute 1 pie crust dough,(see index) in place of cornbread. Cut 3 air vents into the center of the dough about ½ inch each. Replace the chicken with 2 cups of turkey. Replace the peas with green beans, asparagus or okra (14 to 16 oz) Replace the carrots with squash or diced tomatoes, (14-16 oz)

CORNBREAD BATTER

1 tablespoon of vegetable oil
1½ cup of cornmeal
¼ cup of flour
1½ teaspoon of baking powder
1 teaspoon of sea salt
1 tablespoon of sugar
1 large egg
1½ cups of buttermilk

Preheat oil in a baking dish at 400 degrees. Combine the next 5 ingredients. Next add the egg into the dry mixture and stir. Follow with the buttermilk and mix well. Pour batter over oil in a medium size baking dish. Bake for 30-45 minutes or until golden brown.

CLAM CHOWDER

2 ½ cups of potatoes, peeled, diced
2 lbs of little neck clams, cleaned (15 to 20 clams)
1 cup of white wine
4 cups of chicken stock,(see index)
½ cup of beef bacon, chopped
1 large onion, diced
3 stalks of celery, diced
1 cup of carrots, diced
3 garlic cloves, minced
¼ cup of flour
¼ teaspoon of cayenne pepper
1 cup of milk
¼ cup of butter
1 teaspoon of thyme
½ teaspoon of basil
½ teaspoon of oregano
1 cup of cream
½ teaspoon of sea salt
½ teaspoon of white pepper
1 teaspoon of parsley

Cook potatoes in a stockpot until fork tender. Drain and set aside.

Wash clams and place in a large saucepan. Add wine, and 1½ cups of stock. Cook over medium high heat for 2 minutes. Reduce the heat to medium low and simmer until clams open.(Discard any clams that do not open.) Strain and remove cooked clams from shells. Chop and set aside. Save the stock mixture.

Cook bacon in a medium saucepan over medium heat until crisp. Remove bacon and set aside. Place onion, celery, carrots in saucepan and cook until tender, 8 to 10 minutes. Add garlic and sauté for two minutes. Return bacon and add 1½ cups of clam stock. Increase the heat to medium high. Mix ½ cup of stock with flour. Whisk well. Add to the saucepan, stirring continuously and bring to a boil for two minutes. Reduce heat to medium low, add the cayenne pepper, potatoes, milk, butter, thyme, basil, oregano and simmer for 15 minutes. Add the clams and cream. Stir and simmer 10 additional minutes. Add more cream if needed. Season with salt, white pepper, Garnish with parsley.

Variation 1) Substitute 16 oz of shucked clams

COBY CHEESE & ITALIAN SAUSAGE STUFFED BREAST

4 chicken breast, boneless, skinless
2 sheets of wax paper
¼ teaspoon of sea salt
¼ teaspoon of ground black pepper
½ cup of Coby Cheese, (grated)
Italian Sausage stuffing, (see index)
2 eggs, beaten
2 tablespoons of water
1 cup of flour
2 cups of cracker crumbs
¼ cup of olive oil
cooking twine

Preheat oven to 400 degrees.

Wash and flatten the chicken between sheets of wax paper until about ¼ inch thick with meat mallet. Season with salt and black pepper. Spread a layer of Coby cheese over the chicken. Follow with a layer of Italian sausage stuffing over the chicken leaving ¼ inch borders. Fold the bottom over the stuffing. Tuck the sides and roll into a log. Tie with cooking twine.

In a bowl beat eggs together with water. Roll breast in flour. Dip in the egg mixture followed by the crumbs. Repeat with the other breast. Heat ¼ cup of oil in a saucepan over medium heat. Add the 2 breasts and cook until golden brown,(about 2 minutes on each side). Remove the breast and place on a baking sheet. Add additional oil if needed and repeat with the other breast. Bake for 15 to 17 minutes. Remove and cool for 5 minutes. Remove cooking twine. Serve immediately.

VARIATIONS substitute 1) mozzarella cheese and slice of portabella mushroom for the stuffing, 2) seafood dip,(see index), for the stuffing, 3) Mesquite Smoke Salmon, (see index) for stuffing 4) Seafood & Beef, (see index), for stuffing 5) Italian Sausage, and Wild Rice (see index) for a stuffing or 6) Wild Rice and Mushrooms, (see index).

CUBAN BEEF KABOB

1 pound of beef, (cut into 1-inch cubes)
Cuban Garlic Marinade, (see index)
½ green bell pepper, (cut into chunks)
½ red bell pepper, (cut into chunks)
1/3 pint of cherry tomatoes
½ pound of fresh mushrooms

Preheat grill.

Cut beef into 1 inch cubes and marinade for 1 hour. Place beef and vegetables on 8 (8 to 10 inch) metal skewers. Grill kabobs for 3 to 5 minutes on each side and remove, Brush occasionally with the marinade.(Be sure to place the meat about 3 to 5 inches from the coals). Serve over rice.

CURRY BEEF & WILD RICE WITH MUSHROOMS

2 cups of beef chuck, diced
6 scallions, chopped
1 tablespoons of ginger root, minced
½ teaspoons of sea salt
2 tablespoons of peanut oil
1 teaspoon of curry powder
1 tablespoon of sugar
2 tablespoons of red wine
1 ½ cup of beef stock, (see index)
1 teaspoon of cornstarch
4 tablespoons of water
wild rice & mushrooms, (see index)

Sauté beef, scallions, ginger root, salt and oil together over medium high heat for 3-5 minutes. Add the curry powder, sugar, red wine and sauté for 2 additional minutes. Add the beef stock and reduce the heat to medium low. Simmer for 15 minutes. Remove beef and set aside. Increase heat to medium high and bring to a boil. Mix the cornstarch and water. Pour this in with the sauce mixture and stir continually until it thickens. Return the beef to the sauce reduce the heat stirring occasionally. Remove from the heat and serve over wild rice & mushrooms.

FRENCH TOAST

2 eggs
1 cup of milk
1 teaspoon of nutmeg, (ground)
1 teaspoon of cinnamon, (ground)
1/4 teaspoon of sea salt
½ teaspoon of vanilla
1 tablespoon of olive oil
4 slices of French bread
Blueberry Syrup, (see index)

Beat together eggs and milk. Add the next 4 ingredients and whisk well. Heat the oil in a saucepan over medium high heat. Dip both sides of the bread into the egg mixture. Place the soaked bread into the saucepan. Brown, 3 to 5 minutes on both sides. Remove and repeat the process. Serve with Blueberry Syrup, (see index).

Variations 1) (Substitute 6 slices of regular bread for the French bread. Serve with blackberry syrup, see index)
2) (Use peach pie stuffing as a topping for the French Toast)

GRILL CHICKEN AND OYSTER DRESSING

1 whole chicken, completely deboned
½ teaspoon of curry powder
½ teaspoon of garlic powder
½ teaspoon of ground black pepper
½ teaspoon of paprika
8 oz of feta cheese
2 tablespoons of canola oil
2 tablespoons of butter
oyster dressing, (see index)

Preheat oven to 340 degrees.

Wash and season the chicken with curry powder, garlic powder, black pepper, and paprika. Place cheese under the skin of the chicken. In a grill skillet heat oil and butter over medium high heat for 2 minutes. Place chicken in skillet skin side down. Grill the chicken for 8 to 10 minutes on both sides. Remove the chicken drain the oil and place in the oven. Bake at 340 degrees for 45 minutes. Remove and cool for 10 minutes. Slice into ¼ inch strips. Serve with oyster dressing.

GRILLED SALMON WITH STEAMED ASPARAGUS PEARS AND RASPBERRY SAUCE

6 slices of Colby cheese
3 pears, peeled, cored, & quartered
2 cups of white wine
12 asparagus spears, trimmed and steamed
1 cup of water
2 tablespoons of olive oil
1 tablespoon of butter
2 lbs salmon, washed, cut into 4 8oz strips
1/4 cup of teriyaki sauce
2 tablespoons of sugar
1 cup of chicken stock
1 cup of raspberries, (16 to 24)
raspberry sauce, (see index)

Cut 12 (1 inch) circles of Colby cheese and set aside.

Place the pears and wine together in a saucepan over medium high heat for two minutes. Reduce the heat to medium low and simmer for 10 minutes. Remove from the heat and set aside.

Wash asparagus in cold water. Cut the ends and place in a vegetable steamer with one cup of water. Cover and steam 3 to 5 minutes or until tender. Remove from the steamer and place in an ice bath for 1 minute. Remove the asparagus from the ice bath and set aside.

Heat oil and butter in a grill skillet over medium high heat for 2 minutes. Place the salmon and ½ of the teriyaki sauce in the grill skillet skin side down and simmer for 3-5 minutes. Turn over the salmon and add remaining teriyaki sauce. Simmer 3-5 minutes Mix sugar and chicken stock together. Heat in microwave oven for 2 minutes. Add to the grill skillet, reduce heat to low and simmer until absorbed. Remove salmon and set aside.

Place 3 slices of Colby cheese circles together in the center of a plate. Place one fillet over the cheese. Arrange 3 sections of pears around the salmon. Stand 3 asparagus spears over the salmon fillet in a pyramid shape. Place 4 to 6 raspberries around the plate and garnish with raspberry sauce.

ITALIAN SAUSAGE CALZONES

2 tablespoons of olive oil
1 small onion, diced
3 garlic cloves, minced
1 pound of Italian sausage, (casing removed, chopped)
1 teaspoon or oregano
pizza dough, (see index)
3/4 cup of mozzarella cheese, shredded
pizza sauce, (see index)
1 egg, beaten
3 tablespoons of water

Preheat oven to 450 degrees.

Place oil and onion in a saucepan over medium high heat and sauté for 3 minutes. Add garlic, sausage and oregano. Sauté 3 to 5 minutes, or until no longer pink. Remove from the heat, drain and set aside. Allow to cool.

Flour cutting board and cut the dough into 6 equal sections. Roll the dough, (each part) into a 10 to 12 inch circle. Brush excess flour of each side of the dough. Place 1 oz of cheese over the center of the dough. Place two tablespoons of sauce over the cheese. Spoon 1/6 of the sausage mixture over the sauce. Fold the dough over and crimp the edges together, (with a folk). Cut two small vents into the dough. Whisk egg and water together. Brush lightly with the egg wash. Transfer to a cookie sheet. Bake for 15 minutes or until golden brown. Serve immediately.

VARIATIONS 1) Remove Italian Sausage, oregano, pizza sauce Substitute ½ cup of broccoli, add ¼ cup of Parmesan Cheese (Sauté the broccoli, garlic and onion together for 4 minutes. Mix the Mozzarella and Parmesan Cheese together.)
2) Remove Italian Sausage, oregano, pizza sauce. Substitute 3/4 cup of Feta Cheese, crumbled and 1 cup of Spice Tomatoes, (see index).

LASAGNA

1 medium onion, (chopped)
3 garlic cloves, minced
½ cup of mushrooms, sliced
4 tablespoons of olive oil
1 lb ground beef
1 cup of spinach, (washed, drain and chopped)
1 cup of Ricotta cheese
1 egg
¼ teaspoon of white pepper
lasagna sauce, (see index)
8 to 9 lasagna noodles, (cooked according to directions)
1 cup of Mozzarella cheese, shredded
1 cup of Cheddar cheese, shredded
½ cup of Parmesan cheese, grated

Pre-heat the oven to 350 degrees.

In a saucepan add 2 tablespoons of oil over medium heat. Sauté onion, garlic, and mushrooms for 3 to 5 minutes. Add beef and cook until beef is no longer pink. Remove from the heat, drain oil and set aside.

Sauté spinach in 2 tablespoons of oil over medium heat for 3 to 5 minutes. Remove from heat and set aside.

In a bowl whisk together ricotta cheese, egg and white pepper.

Place 1/3 of sauce in the bottom of a deep baking dish. Continue with a layer of lasagna noodles,(cut to fit). Add ½ of the ricotta cheese mixture, ½ of the ground beef and mushroom mixture, ½ mozzarella cheese, and ½ of the cheddar cheese. Add another layer of lasagna noodles, ricotta cheese, ground beef and mushroom mixture, 1/3 sauce, all of the spinach, cheddar cheese and mozzarella cheese. Add another layer of lasagna noodles, sauce, and bake for 40 minutes. Remove from the oven and add the Parmesan cheese.

MOMMA'S GUMBO

3 cups of onions, chopped
3 celery ribs, chopped
2 carrots, chopped
1 small bell pepper, chopped
8 ounces of frozen okra, chopped
6 garlic cloves, minced
2 ounces of canola oil
1 chicken parts, (legs, thighs, breast, and wings)
1 teaspoon of sea salt
1 teaspoon of ground black pepper
1½ cups of butter
2 cups of flour
1 lb of beef smoked sausage, diced
4 large tomatoes, peeled, seeded, diced
1 teaspoon of thyme
1 teaspoon of red pepper flakes
3 bay leaves
2 to 2 ½ quarts of chicken or shrimp stock, (see index)
1 lb of medium raw shrimp, peeled & deveined
8 oz of crab meat
2 ounces of parsley
2 cups of rice

In a skillet sauté onions, celery, carrots, bell pepper, okra, and garlic together with canola oil for 3 to 5 minutes. Remove vegetables and set aside. Add the chicken parts and season with salt and pepper. Cook the chicken until browned. Remove and set aside.

Place 1½ cups of butter in a large stockpot over medium heat. Slowly whisk in flour stirring occasionally until roux becomes smooth and thickens. Use a wooden spoon and continue stirring occasionally until the roux darkens to medium brown. Add sautéd vegetables to the stock pot. Stir continually 3 to 5 minutes. Add chicken, sausage, tomatoes, thyme, red pepper flakes, bay leaves and stock. Bring to a boil stirring occasionally for 3 to 5 minutes, or until thickens. Reduce the heat to medium low and simmer for 30 minutes. Add the shrimp, crap meat and simmer 30 minutes. Stirring occasionally. Remove the bay leaves and season with parsley. Serve immediately over rice.

RICE

2 cups of rice
4 cups of chicken stock, (see index)

Put the rice and stock in a saucepan over medium high heat and bring to a boil. Reduce the heat to low, cover and simmer 3 to 5 minutes, (or until water is absorbed). Serve immediately.

MOO GOO GAI PAN

2 tablespoons of corn oil
½ cup of carrot, (diced)
1 small onion, (sliced)
3 slices of ginger root, (minced)
1 garlic clove, (minced)
2 cups of chicken breast, (cooked and diced)
¼ cup of mushrooms
1 tablespoon of light soy sauce
1/4 teaspoon of black pepper
Mushroom sauce, (see index)
1 cup of cooked rice

In a skillet add oil and sauté carrots, onion, ginger root, garlic over medium high heat for 3 to 5 minutes. Add chicken, mushrooms and soy sauce. Sauté for an additional 3 to 5 minutes. Season with black pepper. Remove from the heat. Add warm mushroom sauce. Serve over rice.

PAN GRILLED GROUPER WITH AVOCADO SALSA

3 lbs of grouper fillets
½ teaspoon of cayenne pepper
½ teaspoon of black pepper
½ teaspoon of sea salt
½ cup of vegetable oil
1 cup of flour
1 ounce of lemon juice
Avocado Salsa, (see index)

Season fillets with cayenne pepper, black pepper, and sea salt. Heat 2oz of oil in a large grill skillet over medium high heat. Lightly coat the fillets with flour. Remove excess flour and grill ½ of the fillets for 3 minutes. Turn the fillets and grill 3 additional minutes, or until golden brown. Remove the fillets and set aside. Repeat the process. Serve with lemon juice and avocado salsa.

PIZZA

Pizza dough, (see index)
1 ½ cup of mozzarella cheese, grated
1 cup of pizza sauce, (see index)
3 ounces of pepperoni, sliced
½ lb of ground beef, (use a teaspoon to scoop, rolled into small balls)
½ cup of mushrooms, sliced
½ yellow bell pepper, (julienne)
½ of diced pineapples
6 ounces of Cheddar cheese, grated
¼ cup of Parmesan cheese

Preheat the oven to 450 degrees.

Dust surface with flour. Roll dough into 2 medium-large circles. Brush off excess flour. Top each circle with ¾ cup mozzarella cheese. Place ½ cup sauce over the cheese. Add ½ pepperoni, beef, mushrooms, bell pepper and pineapple. Bake for 10 minutes. Remove from the oven and add ½ cheddar cheese. Bake another 7 minutes. Remove and sprinkle with Parmesan cheese. (Repeat with other dough, etc . . .)

PORTOBELLO PINWHEEL

6 large flour tortillas
3 lbs of Flank Steak
2 sheets of wax paper
¼ teaspoon of sea salt
¼ teaspoon of ground black pepper
6 slices of mozzarella cheese
2 portobello mushrooms, (sliced)
3 tablespoons of olive oil
11 tablespoon of butter
sweet potato fries, (see index)
cooking twine

Flatten flank steak between sheets of wax paper with a meat mallet until about ¼ inch thick. Season with salt and pepper. Cut into 6 portions. Place a tortilla on a flat surface. Place 1 slice of mozzarella cheese followed by 1/6 of portobello mushrooms leaving a ¼ inch border. Add a flank steak. Fold the bottom over the stuffing. Tuck the sides and roll into a log. Tie with cooking twine. Freeze for 2 hours remove and slice into 3 inch portions. Preheat the oven to 340 degrees. Heat the oil and butter in a saucepan over medium high heat until melted. Pan-fry pinwheel over medium heat until light brown 2-3 minutes. Turn and repeat. Remove from the heat, place on a cookie sheet, and bake in oven for 15 minutes. Remove cooking twine, cool for 5 minutes and serve with sweet potato fries.

Variations 1) (substitute Coby Cheese, Swiss Cheese and American Cheese for the Mozzarella Cheese and portobello mushrooms and do not freeze. Also add ¼ cup of small shrimp).

RAINBOW TROUT STUFFED WITH OYSTER DRESSING

4 (8 ounce) whole rainbow trout
½ teaspoon of sea salt
½ teaspoon of ground black pepper
2 cups of oyster dressing, (see index)
parsley for garnish

Preheat oven to 400 degrees.

Wash and open trout. Season with salt and pepper. Place ¼ cup to 1/3 cup of dressing in each trout. Close and place in large baking dish. Bake 15 to 20 minutes, Remove, and garnish with parsley. Serve immediately

RISOTTO

2 tablespoons of olive oil
1 tablespoon of butter
½ small onion, diced
3 garlic cloves, minced
1 cup of Arborio Rice, (uncooked)
1 cup of white wine
½ cup of mushrooms, sliced
4 to 5 cups of chicken stock, (see index)
1 teaspoon of basil, chopped
1 teaspoon of oregano, chopped
3 ounces of parmesan cheese, (grated)
½ teaspoon of sea salt
½ teaspoon of ground black pepper

Heat oil and butter together in a saucepan over medium high heat. Add onion, basil, oregano and sauté for 3 minutes. Add garlic and sauté for 1 additional minute. Add rice and coat well with the oil and onion mixture. Reduce heat to medium-low, add wine, 1 cup of chicken stock and mushrooms. Simmer until liquid is almost absorbed, stirring occasionally. Add 1 cup of chicken stock stirring constantly until almost absorbed. Repeat the process, adding another cup of chicken stock until rice is tender and creamy. Remove from heat and stir in the cheese. Season with salt, pepper and serve immediately.

SCALLOPS & STEAMED BOK CHOY WITH MANGO SALSA

7 to 9 baby bok choy
½ teaspoon of sea salt
½ teaspoon of ground black pepper
½ small onion, (sliced)
2 carrots, (julienned)
1 ½ cups of water
3 tablespoons of olive oil
1 tablespoon of butter
10 to 12 Scallops
mango salsa, (see index)

Season bok choy with 1/4 teaspoon of salt and 1/4 teaspoon of pepper. Place bok choy, onion, and carrots in a steamer with water. Steam 5 to 7 minutes. Meanwhile, heat oil and butter together in a saucepan over medium high heat. Season scallops with salt and pepper and add to the saucepan. Pan-fry 3 minutes or until light brown on each side and remove. Serve immediately with steamed vegetables and mango salsa.

SHEPHERD'S PIE

Roasted Chicken, (2 to 3 lbs), sliced
1 teaspoon of sea salt
1 teaspoon of ground black pepper
1 orange, (quartered)
3 garlic cloves, minced
1 small onion
2 cups of sweet peas
1 can of carrots, 14.5 to 16 oz
½ cup of chicken stock, see index
Gravy, (see index)
Garlic Mashed Potatoes, (see index)

Pre-heat the oven to 350 degrees. Wash chicken and pat dry with paper towels. Season chicken with salt and pepper. Place the orange slices, garlic, and onion into the chicken cavity. Roast the chicken for 1½ hours. Remove from the oven and allow to cool. Slice chicken breast, legs and thighs. Cover the bottom of a large casserole dish with a layer of chicken, add a layer of peas and carrots. Add ½ cup of chicken stock. Pour gravy over the mixture. Spread a layer of garlic mashed potatoes over the chicken mixture. Bake for 20-30 minutes or until golden brown. Remove, cool 10 minutes.

SHRIMP FETTUCCINE ALFREDO

Pasta dough, (see index)
½ cups of milk
½ cup of cream
2 garlic cloves, minced
1/4 cup of Romano cheese
1/4 cup of grated Parmesan cheese
1 tablespoon of butter
1/4 teaspoon of nutmeg
1 lb of medium shrimp, cooked, peeled, deveined
1/4 teaspoon of sea salt
1/4 teaspoon of white pepper

Prepare pasta dough and let stand for 25 minutes. Roll and cut pasta dough in a pasta machine. Set dough aside. Heat milk and cream together over medium heat. Add garlic and simmer until reduced by 1/3. Slowly whisk in the two cheeses. Remove from the heat. Slowly whisk in butter and nutmeg. Add shrimp and mix well. Season with salt and pepper. Meanwhile cook pasta. Add pasta to boiling water for 3 minutes and drain. Mix well with Alfredo sauce and shrimp.

Variation (Purchase 1lb of pasta and prepare according to directions. Substitute 1 lb of roasted chicken cut into one inch strips for shrimp.)

SHRIMP SCAMPI

4 scallions, chopped
4 garlic cloves, minced
2 tablespoons of olive oil
1 lb of large shrimp, shelled & deveined
½ cup of unsalted butter
½ cup of white wine, (Zolo Chardonnay)
¼ cup of lemon juice
½ teaspoon of crushed red peppers
¼ teaspoon of sea salt
¼ teaspoon of ground black pepper
2 tablespoons of parsley, chopped

Sauté scallions, and garlic together with oil over medium high heat for 2 minutes. Add the shrimp and sauté approximately 2 minutes. Add the butter, wine, lemon juice, red peppers, salt, ground black pepper, and parsley. Stir and reduce the heat to medium low. Simmer until the shrimp turn pink. Remove from heat and serve immediately.

SPAGHETTI

spaghetti sauce
spaghetti
Parmesan Cheese

Spaghetti Sauce

1 large onion, diced
3 stalks of celery, diced
2 tablespoon of olive oil
4 garlic cloves, minced
1 lb of ground beef
½ teaspoon of sea salt
½ teaspoon of black pepper
½ teaspoon of oregano
½ teaspoon of thyme
1 tablespoon of butter
7 or 8 medium tomatoes, peeled, seeded and diced
1 teaspoon of sugar
½ teaspoon of basil
2 1/2 cups of tomato sauce (see index)
½ cup of water

Prepare pasta according to directions, drain and set aside. Sauté onion and celery together with olive oil for 3 minutes in a large saucepan. Add garlic and sauté for 1 minute. Add beef, season with salt and pepper. Cook beef until no longer pink. Drain and add the next 8 ingredients, reduce heat to medium-low and simmer for 30 minutes. (Stirring occasionally) Remove from heat and serve over pasta. Season with Parmesan cheese.
Makes 4 servings

Variation (Omit spaghetti, use four 3oz packages of Beef flavor Ramen Noodles.)

STIR FRIED BEEF

Beef marinade, (see index)
2 cups of beef chuck, slices
1 cup of wild rice
4 tablespoons of peanut oil
1/2 cup of carrots, julienne
1/2 cup of celery, diced
3 green peppers,(seed & diced)
2 teaspoons of ginger root, minced
5 scallions, chopped
2 tablespoons of soy sauce

Marinade the beef slices for 1 hour. Prepare rice according to directions. Remove and set aside. Heat 2 tablespoons of oil over medium high heat in a large saucepan. Sauté carrots, and celery, for 3 to 5 minutes. Add the beef and sauté until no longer pink. Add peppers, ginger root, scallions, soy sauce and sauté an additional 3 to 5 minutes. Remove and serve immediately over rice.

Yields 4 servings

STUFFED BELL PEPPERS

6 large bell peppers
2 cups of chicken stock (see index)
1 cup of rice
2 tablespoons of olive oil
1 large onion, diced
3 garlic cloves, minced
1 lb of ground beef
1 ¼ teaspoon of sea salt
1 ¼ teaspoon of ground black pepper
3 large tomatoes, peeled seeded and diced
½ cup of Shiitake mushrooms, sliced
¼ teaspoon of basil, chopped
1¼ teaspoon of oregano
6 ounces of cheddar cheese, grated
2 cups of spice tomato sauce, (see index)

Preheat the oven to 350 degrees. Cut the tops from the bell peppers. Remove the seeds, and set aside.

Heat the chicken stock in a large stock pan over medium high heat. Bring to a boil add rice and reduce the heat to medium low, Cover and simmer for 5 to 7 minutes or until stock is absorbed. Remove from the heat and set aside.

Heat the oil in a saucepan over medium high heat. Sauté onions and garlic for 3 to 5 minutes. Add beef, season with salt, pepper and cook until no longer pink. Add tomatoes, mushrooms, basil, oregano and cook for an additional 3 to 5 minutes. Remove from the heat and set aside.

In a large bowl combine the cheese with the rice. Add the beef mixture. Stir and mix well. Stuff bell peppers with the mixture. Place the tops back onto the bell peppers. Sit the bell peppers upright in a medium size baking dish. Add tomato sauce. Bake uncovered or 30 minutes, remove and serve immediately.

APPETIZERS

ASIAN CHICKEN FINGERS

2 pounds of chicken breast, boneless & skinless
Asian Marinade, (see index)
1 ½ cup of flour
½ teaspoon of curry powder
½ teaspoon of paprika
½ teaspoon of cayenne pepper
Asian Sauce, (see index)

Cut the chicken into 1½ inch strips. Place the chicken in a plastic bag and marinate in the refrigerator for 2 hours.

Heat Asian Sauce in a saucepan over low heat for 3 to 5 minutes. Cool and use as a sauce for the chicken fingers.

Preheat the oven to 350 degrees. Mix together the flour, curry powder, paprika and pepper in a small bowl. Remove the chicken strips, (discard marinade), and coat them with the flour mixture. Remove excess flour. Place the strips on a baking sheet. Bake for 18 to 22 minutes, (or until golden brown). Remove from the oven and serve with dipping sauce.

BROCCOLI

2 cups of broccoli
½ cup of water
1 tablespoon of butter
¼ teaspoon of sea salt
¼ teaspoon of ground black pepper

Place broccoli in a saucepan of boiling water. Add butter. Steam for 2 minutes and reduce the heat to low. Simmer for 8 addition minutes. Season with salt and pepper.

DADDY'S CHEESE BALL

1 cup of cream cheese
1 cup of Coby Cheese, shredded
2 cups of mozzarella cheese
¼ teaspoon of mustard
1 teaspoon of hot sauce
1 cup of almonds, chopped

Place the first 5 ingredients in a mixer bowl and blend until smooth. Remove, place in a refrigerator and chill for 1 hour. Remove, form in a ball and roll in almonds. Chill for 2 hours. Remove and serve with crackers.

EGG ROLLS

1 egg, beaten
2 tablespoons of water
25 egg roll wrappers
egg roll stuffing, (see index)
Asian Sauce,(see index)
4 tablespoons of peanut oil

In a small bowl whisk egg and water together. Place one tablespoon of stuffing near the end of a wrapper. Pull the end over the stuffing. Fold both sides, roll to the end and seal the wrapper with the egg wash. Repeat the process with the other wrappers. Sauté the egg rolls with oil over medium high heat on all sides for 3 to 5 minutes. Remove, cool and serve with Asian Sauce.

HONEY MUSTARD WINGS

24 chicken wings
½ teaspoon of sea salt
½ teaspoon of black pepper
½ cup of flour
Honey Mustard Sauce, (see index)
3 stalks of celery, (cut into 2 inch strips)
3 carrots, (julienned)

Preheat the oven to 375 degrees. Wash the wings and cut the tips. Season with salt, pepper and lightly cover with flour. Bake the wings for 30 minutes uncovered. Remove the wings and mix with the sauce. Return the wings to the oven and bake an additional 15 to 30 minutes. Serve immediately with celery and carrots.

VARIATIONS 1) Season wings with 1 teaspoon of each 1) garlic powder, paprika, cayenne pepper, sea salt and ground black pepper. Bake for 45 minutes serve with hot wing sauce, (see index). 2) Season with 1 teaspoon of each A) black pepper, B) sea salt and C)½ cup of flour. Preheat the deep fryer to 400 degrees. Fry the wings 7 to 10 minutes or until crispy. Remove the wings drain well. Dip the wings in a sauce (see index). 3)Wash wings and cut tips. Season with salt, pepper and lightly cover with flour. Bake wings for 30 minutes uncovered. Remove wings and mix with Asian Wing Sauce, (see index). Return wings to the oven and bake an additional 30 minutes. Remove and serve immediately.

HONEY MUSTARD WRAPS

4 flour tortillas, (10 or 11 inches each)
honey mustard sauce,(see index)
8 lettuce leaves
8 slices of deli ham
8 slices of deli smoked turkey
4 slices of Coby cheese
4 slices of Cheddar cheese
½ small red bell pepper, (julienned)
1 small tomato, diced
ground black pepper, (to taste)
sea salt, (to taste)

Preheat oven to 350 degrees.

Warm the tortillas in oven for 2 minutes. Remove the tortillas and spread 2 tablespoons of honey mustard sauce on each. Spread leaving 1½ inch borders on all sides. Place 2 leaves of lettuce on each tortilla. Add 2 slices of ham and turkey on each tortilla. Add 1 slice of Coby and Cheddar cheese. Add ¼ of bell peppers, and tomato. Season with pepper. Fold the right and left sides over towards the center. Fold the bottom edge up towards the center. Roll until it is wrapped around the filling. Cut in half and serve immediately.

MELANIE'S COCONUT SHRIMP

6 ounces of cornstarch
¼ teaspoon of cayenne pepper
¼ teaspoon of white pepper
¼ teaspoon of sea salt
6 egg whites
24 medium shrimp, (peeled, and devein)
2 cups of coconut flakes
4 cups of canola oil
pineapple dipping sauce, (see index)

Whisk the cornstarch, cayenne pepper, white pepper, sea salt and egg whites together in a medium-size bowl until foamy. Dip shrimp into batter. Remove and cover with coconut flakes. Repeat with all shrimp. Heat oil to 400 degrees and deep-fry shrimp until golden brown, (approximately 2 to 3 minutes). Remove and drain. Serve with pineapple dipping sauce.

Variation: Replace 24 medium shrimp with 12 large Black Tiger or Gulf Pink Shrimp, (peeled and deveined).

ONION RINGS

1½ cups of all purpose flour
½ cup of corn meal, self-rising
1/4 teaspoon of cayenne pepper
1 teaspoon of onion powder
½ teaspoon of sugar
½ teaspoon of sea salt
1 egg, beaten
1 cup of buttermilk
1 cup of beer
3 large onions, sliced ½ inch thick
4 cups of cooking oil
onion dip, (see index)

Mix together the flour, cornmeal, cayenne pepper, onion powder, sugar and salt together in a large bowl. Whisk together the egg, buttermilk, and beer in a small bowl. Slowly add the buttermilk mixture to the flour mixture. Whisk until smooth. Heat the oil to 375 degrees over medium high heat. Dip the onion rings in the batter. Slowly drop the rings into the hot oil, turning once.(in about 30 seconds.) Deep-fry until golden brown. Remove the onion rings and place on paper towels and drain. Serve immediately with onion dip.

SWEET POTATOES FRIES

5 to7 large sweet potatoes, (rinsed, peeled cut into medium size strips and dry)
4 cups of vegetable oil
1 teaspoon of sea salt
1 teaspoon of white pepper

Heat oil in a large deep saucepan to 400 degrees. Place ¼ of the potatoes into the oil. Fry 8 to 12 minutes or until golden brown and crispy. Remove drain and place the potatoes on several paper towels. Repeat with additional potatoes until completed. Season with salt and pepper to taste.

STUFFED MUSHROOMS

½ cup of chopped spinach,(fresh)
4 tablespoons of olive oil
2 garlic cloves, minced
¼ teaspoon of sea salt
¼ teaspoon of ground black pepper
½ cup of provolone cheese, grated
¼ cup of breadcrumbs
25 large white button mushrooms, (stems removed)
Basil Herb Cream Cheese, (see index)

Preheat the oven to 375 degrees. In a medium skillet sauté the spinach in 2 tablespoons of oil over medium high heat for 3 minutes. Add garlic and sauté for 3 to 5 additional minutes. Remove from heat and place in a medium size bowl. Season with salt and pepper. Add cheese, bread crumbs and mix well. Spoon equal amounts of stuffing on each mushroom. Place the mushrooms on a baking sheet. Drizzle 2 tablespoons of oil over the mushrooms. Bake for 15 minutes. Serve with Basil herb cream cheese.

WONTONS

2 cups of flour, sifted
3 teaspoons of sea salt
1/4 teaspoon of ground cinnamon
1 large egg, beaten, lightly
3 tablespoons of ice water

Mix together flour, 1 teaspoon salt and cinnamon in a large bowl. Add egg and mix well. Add water 1 tablespoon at a time to make the dough. Remove and knead the dough. Return the dough to the bowl, cover with plastic wrap and refrigerate for 1 hour. Remove the dough. Dust cutting board and rolling pin with flour. Roll the dough until paper-thin. Cut the dough into 2½ inch strips and sprinkle with flour. Deep-fry wontons in vegetable oil until golden brown, approximately 2 minutes. Remove, drain, allow to dry and serve.

DESSERTS

APPLE PIE

2 Pie Crust, (see index)

Apple Pie Filling
6 large apples, (peeled, cored and sliced)
½ cup of sugar
½ cup of brown sugar
1/4 cup of flour
1 teaspoon of cinnamon
2 tablespoons of butter

Preheat oven to 350 degrees.

In a large bowl mix apples with the two sugars. Add flour, cinnamon and mix well. Place in pie crust. Cut small pieces of butter into the mixture. Place second crust over pan. Cut and crimp edges. Cut 2 or 3 small vents in the center of pie crust. Bake for 45 minutes. Cool for 10 minutes, Serve immediately.

Variation: Add ½ cup of chopped pitted dates, ½ cup of chopped walnuts, 1 teaspoon of vanilla and 3 eggs slightly beaten in the Apple Pie Filling. Use four pie crust. Use ½ of the mixture for each pie.

GREEN TOMATO PIE

2 Pie Crusts, (see index)

Tomato Pie Filling
3½ cups of green tomatoes, diced
½ cup of granulated sugar
½ cup of brown sugar
¼ cup of flour
1 teaspoon of cinnamon
¼ teaspoon of salt
1 teaspoon of vanilla extract
2 tablespoons of butter

Preheat oven to 350 degrees.

In a large bowl mix tomatoes with the two sugars. In a small bowl combine flour, cinnamon, and salt. Add to the tomato mixture and mix well. Pour filling into the pie crusts. Add drops of extract over the mixture. Cut small pieces of butter into the mixture. Place second crust over the pan. Cut and crimp edges. Cut 2 or 3 small vents in the center of piecrust. Bake for 45 minutes, remove, cool for 10 minutes and serve.

JACK DANIEL'S SWEET POTATO PIE

1/4 cup of raisins
3 tablespoons of Jack Daniel's
3 or 4 large sweet potatoes
3/4 cup of brown sugar
1/4 teaspoon of cinnamon, (ground)
1/4 teaspoon of nutmeg, (ground)
1/4 teaspoon of sea salt
1/4 cup of orange juice
½ teaspoon of vanilla extract
1 tablespoon of butter
pie crust, (see index)

Preheat oven to 425 degrees.

Mix the first two ingredients together in a small bowl for 15 minutes.

Place potatoes in a large stockpot. Cover with water and boil for 45 minutes or until soft. Place peeled potatoes, sugar, cinnamon, nutmeg, and sea salt in an electric mixer bowl. Add the orange juice, vanilla extract, butter and blend until smooth. Pour the Jack Daniel's and raisin mixture in with the potatoes and mix well. Pour the mixture into a pie crust. Place in oven and bake uncovered for 15 minutes. Reduce the heat to 325 degrees and bake an additional 30 minutes.

Variation 1) remove the raisins, Use two ounces of Jack Daniels

MANDARIN ORANGE SORBET

3¼ cups of Mandarin Oranges
1 ounce of orange juice
1 cup of water
1 cup of sugar
¼ cup of corn syrup

Place oranges and juice in a blender and purée mixture. Combine water and sugar in a saucepan over medium heat. Bring to a boil and remove mixture from heat. Stir once and allow to cool. Stir puréed mixture into simple syrup. Add corn syrup and mix well. Pour into a covered container. Place in freezer for 3 or more hours.

MANGO CHEESECAKE

1 cup of mangos,(peeled, cored and diced)
½ teaspoon of almond extract
¼ teaspoon of ground cinnamon
¼ teaspoon of ground nutmeg
1¼ cup of cream cheese, soften
½ cup of sugar
2 eggs
graham cracker crust,(see index)

Preheat the oven to 350 degrees. Boil the mangoes over medium high heat for 5 to 7 minutes, (or until fork tender). Remove from heat, drain and place in a blender. Blend until smooth. Cool and transfer to a large bowl. Add almond extract, cinnamon, nutmeg and mix well. Blend in cream cheese, sugar, eggs until smooth. Pour into crust and bake for 30 minutes. Cool and refrigerate for 3 hours or more.

MANGO FROZEN YOGURT

2 cups of vanilla yogurt
½ cup of whole milk
¼ cup of sugar
1 teaspoon of vanilla
1¼ cup of mangoes, (peeled, pitted, cubed and puréed)

Place yogurt, milk, sugar and vanilla together in a blender and blend for 2 minutes. Slowly add the puréed mangoes. Stir for 1 minute. Pour mixture in a covered container. Place in freezer for 2 or more hours.

PEACH COBBLER

8 tablespoons of butter
1 cup of flour
2 teaspoons of baking powder
3/4 cups of sugar
1/4 teaspoon of sea salt
1 cup of milk
2 cups of peaches, peeled, cored, sliced
½ teaspoon of cinnamon
½ teaspoon of nutmeg

Preheat the oven to 400 degrees. Melt butter in a medium size baking dish and set aside. In a medium bowl, combine flour, baking powder, sugar and salt together. Whisk in milk. Pour the flour mixture over the butter. Spoon the fruit into the mixture. Season with cinnamon and nutmeg. Bake for 30 minutes, (until golden brown) Serve immediately.

Variation 1) Substitute 2 cups of pear for the peaches. Place pears in a plastic bag with ½ cup of brandy. Marinade the pears for 1 hour prior to baking. 2) Substitute 3/4 cups of splenda for sugar, 1 cup of 1 % milk for whole milk.

PEACH PIE

Peach Pie Filling

4 peaches, (peeled, cored, and sliced)
½ cup of granulated sugar
½ cup of brown sugar
¼ cup of flour
1 teaspoon of cinnamon
2 tablespoons of butter
2 pie crust, (see index)

Preheat oven to 350 degrees.

Mix the peaches in a medium size bowl with the two sugars. Add the flour, cinnamon and mix well. Cut small pieces of butter into the mixture. Stir once and place in a deep dish pie crust. Place second crust over the pan. Cut and crimp edges. Cut 2 or 3 small vents in the center of pie crust. Bake for 45 minutes. Cool for 10 minutes. Serve immediately.

PECAN PIE

Pecan Pie Filling

2 cups of corn syrup
6 eggs,(beaten slightly)
2 cups of sugar
4 tablespoons of butter,(melted)
2 teaspoons of vanilla
2 ½ cups of pecans
2 pie crust, page,(see index)

Preheat the oven to 350 degrees. Mix syrup, eggs, sugar, butter and vanilla together in a medium size bowl. Add pecans and mix well. Pour into two regular pie crust. Bake for 55 minutes. Cool for 15 minutes. Serve immediately

RASPBERRY CHEESECAKE

1 cup of frozen raspberries
1 teaspoon of brandy
1 teaspoon of lemon juice
1 teaspoon of orange juice
½ teaspoon of vanilla extract
¼ teaspoon of ground cinnamon
¼ teaspoon of ground nutmeg
2 cups of cream cheese
½ cup plus 1 tablespoon of sugar
2 eggs
graham cracker crust, see index

Place the first 4 ingredients and 1 tablespoon of sugar in a small saucepan over medium high heat. Bring to a boil and reduce the heat to low. Simmer and reduce by ½. Remove from heat and allow to cool. Use as a topping.

Place vanilla extract, cinnamon, nutmeg, cream cheese, ½ cup of sugar and eggs in a mixer bowl. Blend together until smooth. Pour into crust and bake for 30 minutes. Allow to cool, add topping and refrigerate for 2 hours or more.

MARINADES, SAUCES, SALAD DRESSING, ETC....

ASIAN MARINADE

1 cup of soy sauce
½ teaspoon of ginger root, chopped
1 garlic clove, minced
½ cup of brown sugar
½ cup of red wine

Place all ingredients in a small bowl. Mix well, cool for up to 24 hours, use with chicken, fish, etc . . .

ASIAN SAUCE

¼ cup of soy sauce
3 tablespoons of honey
¼ cup of orange juice
1 teaspoon of orange zest
1 teaspoons of ginger, minced
1 tablespoon of Dijon mustard
3 garlic cloves, minced
½ teaspoon of crushed red peppers
¼ teaspoon of sea salt
¼ teaspoon of ground black pepper

Place all ingredients in a medium size bowl and mix well. Baste meat or use as a marinade. Can be stored 3 to 5 days.

ASIAN WING SAUCE

½ cup of marmalade
¼ cup of orange juice
1 tablespoon of soy sauce
½ teaspoon of ginger root, minced
¼ teaspoon of crushed red peppers

Heat the marmalade over medium high heat for 2 minutes. Add the orange juice, soy sauce, ginger root and crushed red peppers. Whisk well. Reduce the heat to low and simmer 3 to 5 minutes. Serve over chicken, beef, lamb, etc . . . Can be stored 3 to 5 days.

BASIL HERB CREAM CHEESE

½ teaspoon of basil leaves, chopped
¼ teaspoon of garlic powder
¼ teaspoon of cayenne pepper
¼ teaspoon of white pepper
½ teaspoon of onion, chopped
¼ teaspoon of oregano leaves, chopped
1 cup of cream cheese

Mix all dry ingredients together. Add cream cheese and blend well. Serve with carrots, celery, crackers, stuffed mushrooms, etc . . .

BÉCHAMEL SAUCE

1¼ cups of milk
¼ onion
1 bay leaf
1 ounce of butter
2 tablespoons of flour
¼ teaspoon of sea salt
¼ teaspoon of white pepper
¼ teaspoon of nutmeg

Over medium low heat simmer the first three ingredients for 14 to 16 minutes in a small saucepan, (Remove onion and bay leaf). In another saucepan melt the butter and whisk in the flour over medium high heat. Using whisk, slowly blend milk in with the flour mixture. Whisk until it thickens stirring occasionally. Season with the pepper, salt, and nutmeg.

BEEF LOG STUFFING

2 tablespoons of olive oil
5 garlic cloves, (minced)
1 bunch of fresh spinach, (about 2 cups)
½ cup of pepper jack cheese

Place oil in a saucepan over medium high heat. Sauté garlic and for 1 minute. Add the spinach and sauté 3 to 5 minutes. Remove from the heat, stir in cheese and cool.

BEEF MARINADE

1 garlic clove, minced
½ cup of soy sauce
2 tablespoons of red wine vinegar
2 tablespoons of brown sugar
1 tablespoon of pineapple juice
1 tablespoon of orange juice

Mix all ingredients together in a medium size bowl. (Can be stored for up to 8 hours in a refrigerator.)

BLUE CHEESE VINAIGRETTE

1 garlic clove, minced
1/3 cup of white wine
1 cup of olive oil
¼ teaspoon of sea salt
¼ teaspoon of ground black pepper
1/3 cup of blue cheese, diced or crumbled

In a blender, purée garlic and wine. Slowly add olive oil, salt, pepper and two tablespoons of blue cheese until mixed well. Pour into a small bowl. Stir in the remaining blue cheese. Serve immediately

BLUEBERRY SYRUP

1 cup of brandy
½ cup of water
1 teaspoon of Balsamic Vinegar
3/4 cups of granulated sugar
1 cup of blueberries

In a small saucepan heat the first 4 ingredients over medium high heat until sugar dissolves, (stirring occasionally). Add blueberries and bring to a boil. Reduce the heat to low and cook until mixture is reduced by ½. Remove from heat, strain and discard berries. Serve over French toast, waffles, etc.

BLACKBERRY SYRUP

1 cup of Brandy
½ cup of water
1 teaspoon of Balsamic Vinegar
¾ cup of granulated sugar
1 cup of frozen Blackberries

Heat the first 4 ingredients over medium high heat until sugar dissolves, (stirring occasionally). Add the blackberries and bring to a boil. Reduce the heat to low and cook until the mixture is reduced by ½. Remove from heat, strain and discard berries.

Serve over French toast, waffles, etc . . .

CHILI OIL

4 garlic cloves, minced
½ cup of olive oil
4 tablespoons of crushed red peppers
¼ teaspoon of sea salt
¼ teaspoon of ground black pepper

In a small skillet heat garlic, crushed red peppers and oil together over medium high heat for 2 minutes. Remove from heat and add salt and pepper. Stir and cool.

CREAMY DRESSING

¼ cup of sour cream
¼ cup of cream cheese
3 tablespoons of red wine vinegar
¼ teaspoon of white pepper

Place all ingredients in blender and blend until smooth. Serve immediately

CUBAN GARLIC MARINADE

¾ cup of lime juice
¼ cup of orange juice
¼ cup of olive oil
1 cup of Cilantro
5 or 6 garlic cloves, (minced)
¼ cup of basil
½ small onion, chopped
½ teaspoon of sea salt
½ teaspoon ground of black pepper
¼ teaspoon of lime zest
¼ teaspoon of orange zest

In a blender combine, lime, orange juice and olive oil. Add cilantro, garlic, basil, onion, salt, pepper, lime zest, orange zest and purée. Refrigerate and marinade meat for 4 or more hours. Good for beef, chicken, and pork.

EGG ROLL STUFFING

1 tablespoon of vegetable oil
2 garlic cloves, (minced)
1 tablespoon of ginger root, (minced)
¾ cup of shrimp, peeled, deveined, (chopped)
¾ cup of ground beef
½ small onion, (chopped)
1 teaspoon of chili powder
1 cup of cabbage, shredded
2 tablespoons of soy sauce
1 tablespoon of sugar
½ cup of shrimp stock, (see index)
¼ teaspoon of ground black pepper

In a saucepan add oil with garlic and ginger. Sauté over medium high heat for 2 minutes. Add shrimp and sauté for 3 minutes or until pink. Remove from heat and set aside.

In a saucepan add beef, onion, chili powder and cook 3 to 5 minutes, (or until no longer pink). Remove from the heat, drain off fat and add to the shrimp mixture.

In a saucepan add cabbage, soy sauce, sugar and shrimp stock. Cook over medium high heat for 7 minutes or until tender. Strain liquid and discard. When cabbage is cool add to the beef and shrimp mixture. Season with black pepper and mix well.

FETA CHEESE VINAIGRETTE

1 cup of olive oil
¼ cup of white wine
1 garlic clove, (minced)
¼ teaspoon of sea salt
¼ teaspoon of ground black pepper
½ cup of feta cheese, crumbled

In a blender purée the first five ingredients together with 2 tablespoons of feta cheese until smooth. Remove from blender and stir in the remaining cheese.

GARLIC MASHED POTATO

2 heads of garlic
2 tablespoons of olive oil
2 lbs of potatoes, (peeled and diced)
½ cup of butter
3/4 cup of heavy cream
¼ teaspoon of white pepper
1¼ teaspoon of sea salt

Preheat the oven to 425 degrees.

Place the garlic on a small baking dish. Drizzle with oil and bake for 40 minutes. Remove and cool for 5 minutes. Squeeze the heads to release the cloves into a mixer bowl.

Place potatoes, 1 teaspoon of salt in a stockpot and cover with water. Cook over medium high heat and bring to a boil. Boil for 10 minutes or until fork tender. Drain the potatoes and place in the bowl with the garlic. Add butter, cream, pepper and salt. Mash and mix until smooth. Serve immediately

GRAVY

1 cup plus 1 tablespoons of chicken stock
1 teaspoon of cornstarch
½ small onion, (diced)
2 garlic cloves, (minced)
2 tablespoons of butter
¼ teaspoon of salt
¼ teaspoon of pepper

In a small bowl stir together one tablespoon of chicken stock, and cornstarch. Set aside. In medium saucepan sauté onion, and garlic cloves with butter over medium high heat for 2 minutes. Add 1 cup of chicken stock and bring to a boil. Pour in cornstarch mixture. Stir constantly until the mixture thickens. Remove from the heat. Season with salt and pepper.

HONEY MUSTARD SAUCE

2/3 cup of Dijon Mustard
4 tablespoons of honey
4 teaspoons of lemon juice
½ teaspoon of garlic powder
½ teaspoons of sea salt

Stir all ingredients together in a small bowl. Serve over chicken wings, carrots, celery, mushrooms, etc . . .

HOT WING SAUCE

½ cup of butter
½ cup of hot sauce
1 tablespoon of honey
1 tablespoon of soy sauce
1 tablespoon of lemon juice
¼ teaspoon of lemon zest

In a small saucepan heat butter and hot sauce together over medium heat until butter is melted. Stir in honey, soy sauce, lemon juice, and lemon zest. Reduce the heat to low and simmer for 3 to 5 minutes. Remove from the heat. Serve with chicken wings, carrots, and celery.

ITALIAN SAUSAGE STUFFING

1 small onion, (diced)
2 garlic cloves, (minced)
1 tablespoon of olive oil
1 cup of Italian Sausage, (casing removed, chopped)
½ teaspoon of oregano, chopped

In a saucepan sauté onion and garlic together with oil over medium high until onion is translucent Add the sausage, oregano and cook until sausage no longer pink, (3 to 5 minutes). Remove from the heat, drain off fat. Allow to cool.

ITALIAN SAUSAGE, WILD RICE AND GARLIC BOK CHOY STUFFING

1 box or 1 cup of wild rice
½ cup of Italian Sausage, (casing removed, chopped)
½ teaspoon of oregano, chopped
4 tablespoons of olive oil
3 garlic cloves, (minced)
3 bunches of bok choy, (chopped)

Prepare rice according to directions on package. Remove from heat and allow to cool.

In a skillet sauté the sausage and oregano together with 2 tablespoons of oil until meat is brown. Remove from heat and allow to cool. Place in a blender and pulse 2 or 3 times and set aside.

In a skillet sauté garlic in 2 tablespoons of oil for 1 minute. Add Bok Choy and cook until tender. Remove from the heat and allow to cool.

In a large bowl combine rice, sausage and bok choy mixtures.

LASAGNA SAUCE

4 cups of diced tomatoes
¼ teaspoon of oregano
1 teaspoon of basil leaves
1 teaspoon of thyme
1 teaspoon of marjoram leaves
1 teaspoon of rosemary, chopped
1 tablespoon of butter
1 teaspoon of sea salt
¼ teaspoon of black pepper

In a blender purée tomatoes together with oregano, basil, thyme, marjoram leaves, and rosemary. Transfer to a saucepan, add the butter, salt and pepper. Simmer for 15 minutes over low heat. (Stir mixture occasionally.) Remove from the heat, and cool.

MESQUITE SMOKED SALMON STUFFING

Mesquite Smoked Salmon
Place 1 (8 oz) salmon fillet in a stove top smoker, skin side down, with mesquite wood chips. Smoke for 15 minutes. Allow to cool for 5 minutes. Remove the skin and flake salmon.

½ cup of cream cheese, (soft)
1 (8 oz) salmon fillet

In food processor stir cream cheese until smooth consistency. Place in small bowl with flaked salmon and mix. Chill for 1 hour.

MUSHROOM SAUCE

1 tablespoons of cornstarch
2 ¼ cups of chicken stock
½ small onion, chopped
1 garlic clove, minced
¼ cup of butter
1¼ cup of mushrooms, sliced
¼ cup of soy sauce
1 teaspoon of curry powder

In a small bowl combine cornstarch, and ¼ cup of chicken stock. In a small saucepan sauté onions and garlic with butter over medium heat until onions are translucent. Add mushrooms, soy sauce, curry powder and mix well. Add 2 cups of chicken stock and increase the heat to medium high. Bring to a boil. Add the cornstarch mixture and stir constantly. Using a whisk blend into sauce. Cook 2 to 3 minutes or until thickened. Remove from heat. Serve over chicken, etc.

OYSTER DRESSING

1 small onion, diced
3 stalks of celery, diced
½ of a large bell pepper, seeded, diced
2 tablespoons of canola oil
3 garlic cloves, minced
2 cups of day old white bread, diced
2 ½ cup of corn bread
1½ cup of oysters, shucked, chopped
3 cups of chicken stock, (see index)
½ teaspoon of sea salt
½ teaspoon of ground black pepper
½ teaspoon of cayenne pepper
½ teaspoon of paprika
½ teaspoon of sage leaves

Preheat oven to 350 degrees.

In a small skillet sauté onion, celery and bell pepper with oil over medium heat until soft. Add garlic and heat for 2 minutes. Remove from the heat. In a large bowl combine breads, oysters and chicken stock. Add onion mixture, salt, peppers, paprika, sage and mix well. Pour into a medium size baking dish, cover with aluminum foil and bake at 350 degrees for 30 minutes. Remove foil and bake 20 to 30 additional minutes.(serve with chicken, trout, turkey, etc . . .)

Variation Do not add the oysters and serve as cornbread dressing

PESTO

½ cup of pine nuts
4 garlic cloves
1 cup of basil, (chopped)
½ cup of olive oil
½ cup of parmesan cheese, (grated)
¼ teaspoon of sea salt
¼ teaspoon of ground black pepper

Place the pine nuts, garlic, and basil into a food processor or blender. Drizzle in the oil and purée. Remove the mixture and place in a small bowl. Add the cheese, salt, pepper, and mix well. Use immediately

PINEAPPLE DIPPING SAUCE

1½ cups of cream cheese
1 teaspoon of ginger root, (minced)
½ teaspoon of vanilla flavor
¼ cup of crush pineapples
¼ cup of coconut milk
½ teaspoon of coconut
1 teaspoon of brandy
1½ cups of honey

In a blender purée the first seven ingredients together. Add honey and pulse to combine. Serve with Melanie's Coconut Shrimp.

PIZZA SAUCE

1 large onion, (diced)
4 garlic cloves, (minced)
¼ cup of olive oil
6 cups of tomatoes, (peeled, seeded, and diced)
½ cup of tomato sauce
½ cup of water
1 teaspoon of oregano
1 teaspoon of basil
1 teaspoon of thyme
1 teaspoon of sea salt
1 teaspoon of ground black pepper

In a large saucepan sauté onion, garlic and oil over medium heat until the onion is translucent. Add the next 8 ingredients and reduce the heat to low. Simmer for 30 minutes, Stir occasionally. Remove from heat and serve immediately.

PIZZA SAUCE (FOR CALZONES ONLY)

1 medium onion, (diced)
2 garlic cloves, (minced)
1 tablespoon of olive oil
½ cup of tomato sauce
½ cup of water
½ teaspoon of oregano
1 teaspoon of basil
½ teaspoon of thyme
3¼ cup of tomatoes, (peeled, seeded, and diced)
½ teaspoon of sea salt
½ teaspoon of ground black pepper

In a medium saucepan sauté onion, garlic and oil together over medium high heat until the onion is translucent. Add the next 8 ingredients and reduce the heat to low. Simmer for 30 minutes, stir occasionally. Remove from the heat, serve immediately.

RASPBERRY SAUCE

¼ cup of raspberries
¼ cup of honey
¼ cup of orange juice
1 teaspoon of orange zest

In a small saucepan whisk all ingredients over medium high heat and bring to a boil. Reduce the heat to low, simmer until mixture is reduced by 1/3. Stirring occasionally Serve immediately.

SEAFOOD AND BEEF STUFFING

½ cup of small shrimp, peeled, (minced)
3 garlic cloves, (minced)
1 tablespoon of olive oil
½ cup of crab meat, chopped
½ teaspoon of red pepper flakes
½ teaspoon of curry powder
½ pound of ground chuck
½ teaspoon of ground black pepper
½ cup of cream cheese, (softened)

In a medium saucepan sauté shrimp, and garlic together with oil for 2 minutes on medium high heat. Add the crab meat, red pepper flakes and curry powder. Sauté for 3 additional minutes. Remove from the heat and set aside.

In a small saucepan brown ground chuck over medium high heat until no longer pink. Remove from the heat, and drain off fat. Allow to cool. In a blender or food processor combine, ground chuck, black pepper and shrimp crab mixture and pulse 2 or 3 times. Add the cream cheese and mix well.

SPICE TOMATOES

3 large tomatoes, (seeds and jelly removed, diced)
1 garlic clove, (minced)
2 tablespoons of olive oil
1 teaspoon of basil
1 teaspoon of oregano
1 teaspoon of thyme
1/4 teaspoon of sea salt
1/4 teaspoon of ground black pepper

In a medium size bowl combine all ingredients together. Serve immediately.

TOMATO STUFFING

2 medium size tomatoes, (seeded, chopped)
½ cup of cracker crumbs

Mix together and chill.

WILD RICE & MUSHROOMS

1 cup of wild rice
½ cup of shiitake mushrooms, sliced
¼ cup of butter
3 cups of water
1/4 teaspoon of sea salt

In a medium saucepan add 3 cups of water and bring to a boil. Add rice, mushrooms and butter. Cover and reduce the heat to low. Simmer for 10 to 15 additional minutes, or until cooked thoroughly. Season with salt.

WING SAUCE

¼ cup of hot sauce
½ cup of margarine

In a small saucepan melt margarine over medium low heat. Add hot sauce and mix well. Remove from the heat and serve over hot wings or use as a dipping sauce.

PIE CRUST, PIZZA DOUGH, ETC...

GARLIC ROLLS

1 teaspoon of vegetable oil
3 garlic cloves
1 ¼ cup of warm water
2 packs of fast rising yeast
1/3 cup of sugar
1 teaspoon of sea salt
4 cups of flour
2 eggs, beaten
1/3 cup of shortening
garlic butter

Preheat the oven to 400 degrees. Drizzle oil over garlic and bake in oven for 20 minutes. Squeeze out the garlic and set aside.

Dissolve yeast in warm water, (Allow to rest for 15 minutes or more.). Add sugar, salt, garlic and 2 cups of flour. Mix well. Add eggs and shortening. Slowly add additional flour and mix to a softened dough. Cover with plastic wrap and let rise for 10 minutes. Knead on a floured surface until smooth and elastic. Place in a greased bowl. Cover and let rise again until it doubles in size. Refrigerate. Remove from the refrigerator at least 2 hours before use. Divide into 8 rolls. Bake at 375 degrees in the oven for 12 to 15 minutes. Brush rolls with garlic butter and serve immediately.

GARLIC BUTTER

8 tablespoons of butter
½ teaspoon of garlic powder

In a small saucepan melt the butter over medium heat. Add garlic powder and whisk well. Remove from the heat. Brush on hot rolls from oven.

GRAHAM CRACKER CRUST

(makes one pie crust)
1 cup of graham crackers, crumbs
3 tablespoons of sugar
3 tablespoons of butter, (melted)

Preheat the oven to 325 degrees. Mix all the ingredients together in a small bowl. Pour and press onto the bottom of a 9 inch pan. Bake for 10 minutes and allow to cool.

PASTA DOUGH

2 cups of flour
2 teaspoons of sea salt
3 large eggs
1 tablespoon of olive oil
1 tablespoon of water

Place flour and 1 teaspoon of salt in a mixer with a dough hook. Add eggs mixing on low. Slowly add olive oil. Add water. (Add more water if it's too dry.) Remove dough and add a little flour if too wet. Wrap dough with plastic wrap and allow to rest at room temperature for 25 minutes. Cut pasta into quarters and roll through the pasta rollers. Reduce,(adjust) the number on the machine and repeat the process. Continue until setting is 1 or 2. (Repeat the process with additional dough.) Cut the spaghetti, fettuccine, etc . . . Allow pasta to dry for 1 hour. Add the pasta to simmering water with 1 teaspoon of salt. Stir with tongs. Cook pasta for about 60 seconds and drain.

PIE CRUST, (1 PIE CRUST)

1¼ cup of flour
2 teaspoons of sugar
1/4 teaspoon of sea salt
4 tablespoons of butter
1 egg yolk
2 teaspoons of lemon juice
4 or 5 teaspoons of cold, (ice water)
plastic wrap

In a large bowl stir together flour, sugar and salt. Cut the butter into the flour mixture. Add the egg yolk, lemon juice and mix together. Add the water a tablespoon at a time forming a ball. When the dough sticks firmly together stop adding the water. Cover with plastic wrap and chill for 1 hour.

Remove and roll the dough on floured surface to fit the pan. Wrap the dough around the rolling pin and cover the pan, (unwind). Cut and crimp edges.

PIE CRUST, (2 PIE CRUST)

3 cups of flour
1 tablespoon of sugar
½ teaspoon of sea salt
8 tablespoons of cold butter
1 egg yolk
1 tablespoon of lemon juice
4 to 5 tablespoons of cold, (ice water)
plastic wrap

In large bowl combine the first three ingredients together. Cut butter into the flour mixture. Add the egg yolk, lemon juice and mix. Add the water a tablespoon at a time forming a ball. When the dough sticks firmly together stop adding the water. Cover with plastic wrap and chill for 1 hour. Cut the dough in half. Roll the first half on a floured surface to fit a 9 inch pie dish. Wrap around the rolling pin and cover the dish with the dough, (unwind). Cut the edges and add the pie filling.

Roll the second half of dough also to fit 9 inch pie dish. Wrap around the rolling pin and cover the dish. (unwind) Cut and crimp edges. Cut 3 or 4 (½ inch) vents to allow the steam to escape.

PIZZA DOUGH

½ ounce of yeast
1 cup of warm water
2 1/2 cups of all purpose flour
1 teaspoon of sea salt
1 tablespoons of olive oil

In a medium size bowl place yeast in the water and allow to stand for 15 minutes. In another bowl combine flour and salt. Using dough hook with the mixer on low slowly add dry ingredients to yeast mixture. Slowly add to live oil,(add additional oil if needed). Dough is ready when it pulls away from sides of bowl. Form dough in a ball and place in the bowl. Cover with plastic wrap and allow to rise for 1 hour. Remove the dough and transfer to a cutting board. Place a little flour on the board and rolling pin. Divide dough in half and make 2 balls. With rolling pin roll in a circle and place on pizza pan. (Repeat with 2nd ball for 2nd pizza if needed.)

STOCKS

BEEF STOCK

2 lbs of beef bones, (ribs, skin)
1 carrot, chopped
2 celery stalks, chopped
½ medium onion, diced
6 peppercorns
1 teaspoon of sea salt
1 bay leaf
2 garlic cloves
2 quarts of water

Place all ingredients in a medium size stockpot over medium high heat. Bring to a boil. reduce heat to low and simmer for 1 hour. Strain, remove fat, cool and refrigerate or freeze.

CHICKEN STOCK

8 cups of water
2 stalks of celery, (diced)
½ onion, (diced)
2 carrots, (diced)
chicken parts, (backs, neck, bones, livers, neck, gizzard etc . . .)
8 peppercorns
1 bay leaf
6 garlic cloves
1 teaspoon of sea salt

Combine all ingredients in a stockpot. Cover with water over medium high heat and bring to a boil. Reduce the heat to low and simmer for 45 minutes. Strain, remove the fat, and season with salt. Cool and refrigerate.

SHRIMP STOCK

3 lbs shrimp shells
1 cup of shrimp
½ onion, (chopped)
2 celery ribs, (chopped)
2 carrots chopped
1 1/2 quarts of water
1 tablespoon of sea salt

Place shrimp shells, shrimp, onion, celery, carrots and water in a stock pot over medium high heat and bring to boil. Reduce the heat to low, season with salt and simmer for 30 minutes. Remove from the heat and strain.

SALSA, DIPS, ETC...

AVOCADO SALSA

2 avocados, (peeled, seeded, diced)
2 tomatoes, (jellies and seeds removed)
1 small onion, (diced)
1 bell pepper, (seeded, diced)
1 jalapeno, (seeded and chopped)
¼ cup of lime juice
1 bunch of cilantro, (stems removed, chopped)
2 tablespoons of olive oil
1/4 teaspoon of ground black pepper
1/4 teaspoon of sea salt

In a medium size bowl mix together the avocados, tomatoes, onion, bell pepper, jalapeno, lime juice and cilantro. Place in a refrigerator and chill for 30 minutes. Remove and add oil, pepper, salt and stir. Serve immediately

FRUIT SALSA

1 mango, (peel, seeded, and chopped)
1 papaya, (peel, seeded, and chopped)
1 red chili, (seeds and veins removed, chopped)
2 to 3 tablespoons of cilantro, (chopped)
1 teaspoon of lime zest
¼ cup of lime, juice
¼ teaspoon of sea salt
¼ teaspoon of ground black pepper

In a medium size bowl combine mango, papaya, chili pepper and cilantro. Add zest, lime juice, salt, black pepper and stir. Chill in refrigerator for 1 hour before serving. Good with fish, and chicken,

MANGO SALSA

1 large mango, (peeled, seeded and diced)
2 medium tomatoes, (seeded and diced)
4 scallions, (chopped)
¼ teaspoon of crushed red peppers
¼ cup of cilantro, (finely chopped)
4 tablespoons of lime juice
½ teaspoon of ground cumin
2 tablespoons of olive oil
¼ teaspoon of sea salt

In a medium size bowl combine mango, tomatoes, scallions, crushed red peppers, cilantro, and lime juice. Add the cumin, olive oil, salt and mix well. Cover and chill in refrigerator for 1 hour.

TOMATO SALSA

6 to 8 tomatoes, (peeled, seeded and diced)
1 large onion, (diced)
½ cup of cilantro, (chopped)
2 Serrano chili peppers, (seeds and veins removed, and chopped)
1 teaspoon of lime zest
1 teaspoon of lime juice
½ teaspoon of light brown sugar
½ teaspoon of sea salt
3 tablespoons of olive oil

In a medium size bowl mix together tomatoes, onion, cilantro, chili peppers, lime zest, and lime juice. Place in a refrigerator and chill for 30 minutes. Remove, add sugar, salt, olive oil and stir. Serve immediately

SEAFOOD DIP

1 tablespoon of butter
1 tablespoon of olive oil
½ small onion, diced
2 garlic cloves, (minced)
½ cup or plain yogurt
½ cup of cream cheese, soften
1 teaspoon of crushed red peppers
¼ teaspoon of sea salt
¼ teaspoon of ground black pepper
1 cup of crab meat, chopped
1 cup of shrimp, small
¼ cup of bread crumbs
¼ cup of Parmesan Cheese Grated

In a small skillet melt butter with oil over medium high heat. Add onion and sauté until translucent. Add garlic, sauté for additional 2 minutes. Remove from the heat and drain oil.

Preheat oven to 400 degrees. In blender mix yogurt, and cream cheese together until smooth. Place in a mixing bowl. Add onion, garlic, crushed red peppers, salt, pepper, and mix well. Gently with spatula fold crabmeat, shrimp and bread crumbs into the mixture. Place the mixture in a dish and bake for 10 minutes. Remove and top with Parmesan cheese. Bake for 3 additional minutes and remove.

ONION DIP

½ cup of dried onions
3 minced garlic cloves
¼ cup of grated carrot
1 teaspoon of basil
¼ teaspoon of white pepper
¼ teaspoon of sea salt
2 cups of sour cream

Mix all ingredients together in a medium size bowl. Chill in refrigerator for 1 hour. Serve with crackers, chips, carrots, radishes, and celery.

SPINACH DIP

1½ cup of sour cream
6 ounces of cream cheese, (softened)
1½ cups of chopped spinach
5 scallions, chopped
3 garlic cloves, minced
1 teaspoon of carrot, (grated)
½ teaspoon of basil leaves, (chopped)
¼ teaspoon of celery seed
¼ teaspoon of sea salt
¼ teaspoon of ground black pepper

Whisk together the sour cream and cream cheese. Stir in the next eight ingredients. Chill in refrigerator for 1 hour. Remove and serve immediately

SOUP, SALADS, ETC...

CHEDDAR CHEESE SOUP

2 tablespoons of flour
2 cups of chicken stock, plus six tablespoons (see index)
2 tablespoons of butter
1 tablespoon of olive oil
½ small onion, diced
½ red bell pepper, diced
1 carrot, diced
½ cup of heavy cream
½ cup of cheddar cheese
¼ teaspoon of white pepper
¼ teaspoon of sea salt

In a small bowl mix flour and six tablespoons of chicken stock.

In a large saucepan heat butter and oil together over medium heat. Add the onions, bell peppers, carrots and sauté for 4 to 5 minutes. Slowly add chicken stock and bring to a boil. Add the flour mixture and whisk until the stock thickens. Remove, place in a blender on purée until smooth. Return the soup to a saucepan on low heat. Whisk in the cream and ½ of the cheese until cheese is melted. Add the remaining cheese and whisk until it is melted. Season with white pepper and salt.

EGG DROP SOUP

1 tablespoon of cornstarch
4 ½ cups of chicken stock, (see index)
3 tablespoons of soy sauce
½ cup of scallions, chopped
½ cup of button mushrooms, (sliced)
2 eggs, lightly beaten
¼ teaspoon of white pepper
salt to taste
wontons, (see index)

Mix cornstarch and ½ cup of chicken stock together and set aside.

In a large saucepan heat 4 cups of chicken stock over medium high heat. Bring the mixture to a boil. Add soy sauce, scallions, mushrooms. and boil for 2 minutes. Slowly add the cornstarch mixture while stirring. Stir until mixture thicken and reduce heat to low. Slowly add the eggs and stir. Simmer for 3 to 5 minutes. Season with salt and pepper. Serve immediately with wontons.

THREE BEAN SOUP

½ cup of pinto beans
½ cup of lima beans
½ cup of northern beans
6 cups of water
5 peppercorns
3 thyme sprigs, (wrapped in cheesecloth)
2 teaspoons of sea salt
1 tablespoon of unsalted butter
2 tablespoons of olive oil
1 small onion, diced
3 garlic cloves, minced
1 tablespoon of flour
½ cup of chicken stock, (see index)

In a large stockpot add dried beans, water, peppercorns, and thyme sprigs. Cook over medium high heat and bring to a boil. Add 1 teaspoon of salt and reduce the heat to medium low. Cover and simmer for 1½ hours. Add additional water as needed. Stir the beans occasionally. Remove from the heat and drain. (Remove cheesecloth.) Save the liquid. Remove 1 cup of beans, add three tablespoons of the liquid and purée in blender until smooth.

In a small saucepan melt butter and oil together over medium high heat. Add onion, and sauté until translucent. Add garlic and sauté for 2 additionally minutes. Coat with flour and slowly add the chicken stock. Bring to a boil, whisk constantly until mixture thickens. Remove from the heat. Add to the stockpot with beans along with purée mixture and 1 teaspoon of salt. Heat, stir and serve hot.

BROCCOLI, APRICOT, ALMOND SALAD

1 cup of broccoli, (washed and chopped)
½ cup dried apricot quarters
¼ cup of raisins
¼ cup of almonds
1 Bartlett pear, (peel and core the pear, diced)
1 teaspoons of fresh basil, chopped
¼ teaspoon of ground black pepper
¼ teaspoon of sea salt
creamy dressing, (see index)

Mix broccoli, apricots, raisins, almonds, pear and basil together in a medium size bowl. Season with salt and pepper. Serve with creamy dressing.

FRUIT SALAD

½ cantaloupe, (peeled, seeds removed, and diced)
½ honeydew melon, (peeled, seeds removed, diced)
1 cup of seedless grapes
½ cup of raspberries, (sliced)
½ cup of blueberries
1 pear, (peel and core the pear, diced)
1 cup of peach yogurt

Mix the cantaloupe, honeydew melon, grapes, raspberries, blueberries, and pear together in a medium size bowl. Stir in the yogurt and chill in refrigerator for 1hour. Serve immediately.

SPINACH SALAD WITH FETA CHEESE VINAIGRETTE

2 bunches of spinach, (washed, stems removed)
1 small can of mandarin orange slices, (drained)
1/4 cup of walnuts, (chopped)
¼ teaspoon of sea salt
¼ teaspoon of white pepper
Feta Cheese Vinaigrette, (see index)

Mix together the spinach, mandarin orange slices and walnuts. Season with salt and pepper. Serve with feta cheese vinaigrette.

SPINACH SALAD WITH GRILLED HALIBUT AND BLUE CHEESE VINAIGRETTE

3 tablespoons of canola oil
1lb of Halibut
¼ teaspoon of sea salt
¼ teaspoon of ground black pepper
1 bunch of spinach, (washed, stems removed)
2 Bartlett pears, (peel and core the pear, quartered)
¼ cup of almonds
½ cup of croutons
Blue Cheese Vinaigrette (see index)

Heat canola oil in a grill skillet over medium high heat. Season halibut with salt and pepper. Place halibut into skillet and grill on both sides 3 to 5 minutes. Remove, (set aside and cool. Cut into 8 (2 oz strips).

Mix together the spinach, pears, almonds and croutons in a large bowl. Add the halibut and blue cheese vinaigrette. Serve immediately.

TOPPINGS

APPLE TOPPING

2 cups of apples, (peeled, cored, slice)
3 tablespoons of lemon juice
½ teaspoon of lemon zest
1/3 cup of brown sugar
1 teaspoon of vanilla extract
3 tablespoons of brandy

In a medium size bowl combine apple slices, lemon juice, and lemon zest. Allow to rest for 3 to 5 minutes. Add the sugar, vanilla extract, brandy and mix well. Serve over ice cream, pork chops, waffles or use as a pie filling.

RASPBERRY CHEESECAKE TOPPING

1 cup of frozen raspberries
1 teaspoon of brandy
1 teaspoon of lemon juice
1 teaspoon of orange juice
1 tablespoon of sugar

Place all ingredients in a medium size saucepan over low heat. Simmer and stir until sugar dissolves. Remove from heat and allow to cool. Use as a topping for cheesecake, waffles, etc . . . .

INDEX

Appetizers 41
Apple Pie 52
Apple, Date Pecan Pie 58
Apple Topping 104
Asian Chicken Fingers 42
Asian Marinade 61
Asian Sauce 61
Asian Wing Sauce 62
Avocado Salsa 92
Basil Herb Cream Cheese 62
Béchamel Sauce 63
Beef Cheese Quiche 11
Beef Log 12
Beef Log Stuffing 12
Beef Marinade 64
Beef Stew 13
Beef Stock 89
Blackberry Syrup 65
Blue Cheese Vinaigrette 64
Blueberry Syrup 65
Bow Tie Pasta, Peppers and Meatballs 14
Breakfast Quesadilla 15
Broccoli 43
Broccoli, Apricot, Almond Salad 100
Cheddar Cheese Soup 97
Chicken Pot Pie 16
Chicken Stock 89
Chili Oil 66
Clam Chowder 18
Coby Cheese & Italian Sausage Stuffed Breast 19
Cornbread Batter 17
Creamy Dressing 66
Cuban Beef Kabob 20
Cuban Garlic Marinade 67

Curry Beef & Wild Rice with Mushroom 21
Daddy's Cheese Ball 43
Dessert 51
Egg Drop Soup 98
Egg Rolls 44
Egg Roll Stuffing 68
Feta Cheese Vinaigrette 69
French Toast 22
Fruit Salad 100
Fruit Salsa 92
Garlic Butter 83
Garlic Mashed Potatoes 69
Garlic Rolls 83
Graham Cracker Crust 84
Gravy 70
Green Tomato Pie 53
Grill Chicken and Oyster Dressing 23
Grilled Salmon with steamed Asparagus Pears & Raspberry Sauce 24
Honey Mustard Sauce 70
Honey Mustard Wings 45
Honey Mustard Wraps 46
Hot Wing Sauce 71
Italian Sausage Calzones 25
Italian Sausage Stuffing 71
Italian Sausage, Wild Rice and Garlic Bok Choy Stuffing 72
Jack Daniel's Sweet Potato Pie 54
Lasagna 26
Lasagna Sauce 73
Mandarin Orange Sorbet 55
Mango Cheesecake 55
Mango Frozen Yogurt 56
Mango Salsa 93

Marinades, Sauces, Salad Dressing,
  Etc ... 60
Melanie's Coconut Shrimp 47
Mesquite Smoked Salmon Stuffing 74
Momma's Gumbo 27
Moo Goo Gai Pan 1 28
Mushroom Sauce 74
Onion Dip 95
Onion Rings 48
Oyster Dressing 75
Pan Grilled Grouper with Avocado
  Salsa 29
Pasta Dough 84
Peach Cobbler 56
Peach Pie 57
Peach Pie Filling 57
Pecan Pie 58
Pesto 76
Pie Crust, (1 Pie Crust) 85
Pie Crust, (2 Pie Crust) 86
Pie Crust, Pizza Dough, ETC ... 82
Pineapple Dipping Sauce 76
Pizza 30
Pizza Dough 87
Pizza Sauce 77
Pizza Sauce (for Calzones only) 78
Portobello Pinwheel 31
Rainbow Trout Stuffed with Oyster
  Dressing 32
Raspberry Cheesecake 59
Raspberry Cheesecake Topping 104
Raspberry Sauce 79
Rice 28
Risotto 33
Salsa, Dips, ETC ... 91
Scallops & Steamed Bok Choy with
  Mango Salsa 34
Seafood and Beef Stuffing 79
Seafood Dip 94
Shepherd's Pie 35
Shrimp Fettuccine Alfredo 36
Shrimp, Fish Stock 90

Shrimp Scampi 37
Soup, Salads, ETC ... 96
Stocks 88
Spaghetti 38
Spaghetti Sauce 38
Spice Tomatoes 80
Spinach Dip 95
Spinach Salad with Feta Cheese
  Vinaigrette 101
Spinach Salad with Grilled Halibut and
  Blue Cheese Vinaigrette 102
Stir Fried Beef 39
Stuffed Bell Peppers 40
Stuffed Mushrooms 49
Sweet Potato Fries 49
Three Bean Soup 99
Tomato Pie Filling 53
Tomato Salsa 93
Tomato Stuffing 80
Toppings 103
Wild Rice & Mushrooms 81
Wing Sauce 81
Wontons 50

Get Published, Inc!
Thorofare, NJ 08086
05 November 2009
BA2009248